USBORNE HISTORY

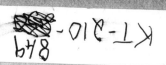
Tudors and Stuarts

Usborne Quicklinks

The Usborne Quicklinks Website is packed with thousands of links to all the best websites on the internet. The websites include information, video clips, sounds, games and animations that support and enhance the information in Usborne internet-linked books.

To visit the recommended websites for this book, go to the Usborne Quicklinks Website at **www.usborne-quicklinks.com** and enter the keywords **History of Britain**, then click on **Tudors and Stuarts**.

When using the internet please follow the internet safety guidelines displayed on the Usborne Quicklinks Website. The recommended websites in Usborne Quicklinks are regularly reviewed and updated, but Usborne Publishing Ltd. is not responsible for the content or availability of any website other than its own. We recommend that children are supervised while using the internet.

Tudors
and
Stuarts

Fiona Patchett, Kate Davies,
Rob Lloyd Jones & Conrad Mason

Illustrated by Ian McNee
Designed by Stephen Moncrieff & Steve Wood
Edited by Ruth Brocklehurst & Jane Chisholm
Consultant: Janice Barter & Dr. Anne Millard

Contents

A golden age

The 16th and 17th centuries were a time of momentous change in Britain. Under the Tudor monarchs, England and Wales were finally united, and the English gained control of parts of Ireland. The Tudors and the Scottish royal family, the Stewarts (later renamed Stuarts) also came together, through a marriage which later brought the two countries under one Stuart king.

It was an age of great religious upheaval, which eventually saw Protestantism replace Catholicism as the official faith in Britain. Many people's views of the world changed dramatically too, as adventurers explored new lands, and the arts and sciences flourished in what became known as a golden age.

This is a portrait of Henry VII and Elizabeth surrounded by York and Lancaster roses.

Henry created a new family emblem, the Tudor rose, by combining the white rose of York with the red rose of Lancaster.

Lancaster rose

York rose

Tudor rose

The first Tudor

In 1485, Henry Tudor defeated King Richard III at the Battle of Bosworth, and became Henry VII, the first Tudor king of England. His victory ended 30 years of bloody civil war between two branches of the royal family – the Lancastrians and the Yorkists. Henry, who was a Lancastrian, brought the two sides of the family together by marrying Elizabeth of York. His reign promised a new period of wealth and stability in the kingdom.

Although he had married Elizabeth, Henry still feared that his Yorkist enemies might try to seize power. To strengthen his position, he took their estates, and had some of them executed for treason. He also brought in high taxes and banned nobles from raising their own armies. If they broke his laws, they were tried in a court, the Star Chamber, and fined heavily.

Plots and pretenders

Henry was right to be suspicious – he faced several Yorkist plots to overthrow him. Often his enemies were helped by the Irish and by the kings of Scotland and France, England's traditional enemies. In 1487, a group of Yorkists persuaded a boy named Lambert Simnel to pretend he was Richard III's nephew, the Earl of Warwick, who they believed had a stronger claim to the throne than Henry did. But the real Warwick was a prisoner in the Tower of London, and Henry paraded him through the streets to prove it. Simnel was arrested and sent to work in the royal kitchens as a punishment.

In 1491, a more serious threat came from a man named Perkin Warbeck, who pretended to be another of Richard III's nephews, Richard, Duke of York. It was thought that the real Richard had been murdered in the Tower of London, but Warbeck claimed that he had escaped from the Tower and fled abroad. He raised an army and invaded England. But he was defeated, and later hanged as a traitor.

James and Margaret

Among Warbeck's supporters was the Stewart king of Scotland, James IV. England and Scotland had often fought in the past, and the Scots sometimes sided with the French against England. But when Warbeck's plot failed, James decided it was time to make peace with the English.

To prevent further fighting, a treaty was signed, and in 1503, James married Henry's daughter, Margaret. This brought together the Stewart and the Tudor families. But the marriage didn't bring peace for long. Ten years later James IV was killed while fighting the English at the Battle of Flodden.

Tudor society

Henry kept close control over the nobles, but he still needed their support. They

were at the top level of Tudor society.

Nobles were men with titles such as lord, duke and earl. They came from important families, which owned lots of land.

The gentry were wealthy, well-educated, and didn't need to work with their hands for a living. They included rich merchants and knights.

Yeomen farmers owned land, which they worked on themselves.

The lowest classes of society included 'tenant farmers' who rented land, farm workers, servants and beggars. This group made up 90% of Britain's population.

7

Henry VIII

In 1509, Henry VII died and was succeeded by his 18-year-old son, who became Henry VIII. The new King had a huge appetite for pleasure – eating too much, drinking too much, and spending most of the money that his father had saved on grand banquets and arrogant displays of power.

This portrait by Hans Holbein, a German painter, shows Henry in fine clothes and jewels, to show off his wealth and power.

Tudor tantrums

The young King was incredibly athletic, and often challenged the nobles in his court, known as courtiers, to wrestling or jousting competitions. Henry always won, of course – no one dared to beat him. The courtiers lived in constant fear of the King's childish moods. He often flew into sudden rages, thrashing them with sticks or bursting into tears.

As his reign wore on, Henry grew paranoid, believing that his courtiers would betray him, so he encouraged them to spy on each other. He executed some of his most trusted ministers simply because of lies that were spread by their rivals.

As this portrait shows, Henry VIII was an imposing figure of a man. Not only was he broad-chested, but historians believe he could have been as tall as 190cm (6ft, 4inches) at a time when people were, on average, shorter than they are today.

The King's Cardinal

At first, the most powerful minister in the land
was Henry's chancellor, Cardinal Thomas Wolsey.
He wasn't a noble, but he was hard working and
ambitious, and soon became the King's closest advisor.
At the height of his powers, Wolsey owned palaces,
and founded schools and colleges. Many courtiers
hated him for his wealth and his influence over Henry.

Henry's Great Matter

Henry married his brother's widow, Catherine of
Aragon, and they had a daughter, Mary. As Catherine
got older, Henry worried she would never have a son.
The problem became known in court as the King's
Great Matter. In around 1527, Henry fell in love
with one of his courtiers, Anne Boleyn. He wanted to
divorce Catherine so that he could marry Anne, and
have another chance to father a son.

But since England was a Catholic nation, divorces
had to be agreed by the Pope – and he wouldn't allow
it. Henry turned to Wolsey to find a solution. Wolsey
failed, and his enemies pounced. They accused him of
treason, and turned the King against him. Wolsey fell
ill and died in 1530, on his way to face the charges.

The break with Rome

Although Henry was a devout Catholic, he saw that
the only way to get the divorce he wanted was to
break away from the Roman Catholic Church. So he
ordered Parliament and Thomas Cranmer, Archbishop
of Canterbury, to declare him Supreme Head of the
Church in England, instead of the Pope. Now, he
could do whatever he liked.

Henry's six wives

Henry had six wives.
His first marriage,
to Catherine of
Aragon, ended
in divorce.

He had Anne Boleyn
executed on charges of
witchcraft and
adultery, after
she bore him
a daughter,
Elizabeth,
but no son.

Jane Seymour
was Anne Boleyn's
lady-in-waiting.
She died after
giving birth to
a son, Edward.

Henry divorced
his fourth wife,
Anne of Cleves,
deciding that
she was ugly.

He had
Catherine Howard
executed for
having affairs.

Catherine
Parr looked
after the old
King until
he died.

When Henry died in
1547, he spoke the
name of Jane Seymour,
the only wife that he is
said to have truly loved.

Henry's new powers

The Pilgrimage of Grace

Some people were angry with Henry's harsh treatment of the monks. In October 1536, an army of 30,000 people marched from the north of England in protest. It was known as the Pilgrimage of Grace.

Henry promised to consider their grievances, but as soon as the protestors had dispersed, he arrested their leaders and executed them.

Once Henry was in charge of the Church in England, he began using it to increase his own wealth. During the 16th century there were 850 monasteries in England, which were home to over 9,000 monks and nuns. They owned over a quarter of the country's land, which made them very rich. Henry decided to shut them down, and take their money.

The Dissolution of the Monasteries, as it became known, lasted four years, from 1536 to 1540. Led by Henry's new chancellor, Thomas Cromwell, the King's men looted the monasteries, stealing anything of value. Some of the buildings were burned to the ground. Others were simply left to crumble, the valuable lead stripped from their roofs, and beautiful stained glass windows smashed.

This is Fountains Abbey in Yorkshire. It was one of the many wealthy English monasteries that fell into ruin after being closed down.

Wales and Ireland

As well as making himself rich at the expense of the monasteries, Henry extended his power over Wales and Ireland – both Catholic countries. English kings had ruled over Wales for years, and Henry was of Welsh descent. But some areas were controlled by powerful Catholic nobles known as 'marcher lords' who made their own laws and appointed their own officials. Henry worried that after his break with Rome, the marcher lords wouldn't be loyal to him. So, in 1536, he united Wales and England, and brought in English Law for the Welsh.

One of Henry's titles was Lord of Ireland – but in fact he had little power there, and the Catholic Fitzgeralds, the leading nobles in Ireland, often rebelled against him. Henry sent in an army to restore order, and in 1541 he declared himself King of Ireland. But it made little difference. Many Irishmen deeply resented the English claims to their country, and they refused to break with Rome as Henry had done.

Solway Moss

Henry urged his nephew James V of Scotland (James IV's son) to break from Rome. But to his uncle's fury, James refused to do so.

Before long, England and Scotland were at war, and James sent a large army to invade England.

At the Battle of Solway Moss, the Scots outnumbered the English three to one. But they were so disorganized that the English quickly sent them fleeing from the battlefield.

The defeat broke James. He died two weeks later, and the crown passed to his baby daughter, Mary.

In 1520, Henry met Francis I of France at a huge peace conference named the Field of the Cloth of Gold. Everything went well, until Henry challenged Francis to a wrestling match.

Francis won, but the English said that he had cheated. The conference failed to prevent war from breaking out again.

Fortress England

When Henry came to the throne, the most powerful countries in Europe were Spain and France. England and France had always been enemies, and although Henry met the French king for a peace conference, the hostility continued almost throughout his reign.

But, after his break from Rome, Henry grew worried that the Catholic kings of both Spain and France were planning to invade England. So, using the stone from the abandoned monasteries, he built forts along the south coast to protect his country from attack.

The Royal Navy

Before Henry VIII, English kings had borrowed
trading ships for battles, as they didn't have a navy
of their own. But now Henry built up a huge fleet of
ships to protect England.

   The most formidable warship was named *Henri
Grâce à Dieu* – it had five decks and over 200 cannons.
But Henry was fondest of his flagship, the *Mary Rose*.
In 1545, the *Mary Rose* set sail to fight the French.
But it was so overloaded with cannons and men that it
sank, with Henry watching in horror from the shore.

This painting shows Henry's
warship, *Henri Grâce à Dieu*,
leaving England, carrying
the King to the Field of the
Cloth of Gold.

Working in
the fields

Farm workers had to be
ready to do whatever was
asked of them. Their jobs
were different at
different times of year.
The work included:

sowing
seeds...

harvesting
crops...

cutting
back vines...

shearing
sheep...

or building walls
to mark out areas
of land.

The Tudor countryside

While Henry and his troops were busy fighting the
French, most people in Britain lived in rural areas,
and rarely left the villages where they had been born.
All kinds of people lived in the countryside, from
wealthy nobles with large estates, to poor beggars who
lived on village streets. But most country folk were
farmers. They made their living by growing crops and
grazing their animals. The poorest used 'common land'
– land that was free to be used by anyone.

A farmer's life

Farmers spent almost all of their time working outside,
while their wives stayed at home, preparing and
preserving food, baking bread, brewing beer, and taking
care of young children. By the time they were around
seven years old, the children would begin work, too.
Young girls helped their mothers in the house, and
boys joined their fathers in the fields. Everyone had to
work hard to provide food for the family. But however
hard they worked, if the harvest was bad, everyone
went hungry.

For the poorest farm workers, life was much the same
as it had been during the Middle Ages. They lived in
tiny, cold cottages. A few people had small glass
windows, but most had to make do with bits of cloth or
simple wooden shutters to keep out the cold. There was
very little furniture. A table and some stools was all that
most could afford. Often whole families lived together in
a single room, which they shared with their animals –
usually a few chickens, whose eggs they
would sell. If times were hard, the
chickens could be killed and eaten.

Market day

On market day, people set off for the nearest town, with produce to sell. For most, this was the furthest they went from home – roads were bumpy, muddy tracks, and thieves were everywhere. The market was a place to meet friends, attracting everyone in the area. There were also festivals and country fêtes, often on special days, such as Easter and Christmas.

Kett's Rebellion

Meanwhile, life was getting harder for the poorest farmers. In the 1500s, wealthy landowners began fencing off areas of common land for themselves. They wanted to make money by rearing sheep there, and selling wool. This process, called enclosure, left many people with no land to farm. Fences were torn down in protest, and in 1549, a farmer named Robert Kett gathered an army of rebels in Norwich, demanding that the enclosures be pulled down. The rebellion was brutally crushed by the Earl of Warwick.

Fun and games

For rich nobles, the countryside was like a playground. They enjoyed hunting deer with dogs, or bows and arrows...

...and hawking – using trained birds of prey to catch rabbits and pheasants.

This painting shows a fête in the village of Bermondsey.

Rebirth and reform

This is a detail from *The Ambassadors*, by the Renaissance painter Hans Holbein. The men, a merchant and a cleric, are surrounded by instruments of Renaissance learning.

In the middle of the floor, you can see a squashed image of a human skull – a reminder that death comes to everyone.

During the 15th and 16th centuries, a great cultural movement swept across Europe. This became known as the Renaissance – or 'rebirth' – because artists and writers rediscovered ideas from ancient Greek and Roman civilizations, and produced brilliant works of art and literature. At the same time, great thinkers and scientists came up with new ideas and discoveries that gradually changed people's lives.

Renaissance men

In England and Scotland, King Henry VIII and King James IV led the way as 'renaissance men' – well-educated in all fields of art and literature, and dedicated to learning.

Henry played several instruments, wrote music, and spoke French, Latin and Spanish. He invited great painters, like the German Hans Holbein, to the English court.

James was even more impressive. One great scholar of the Renaissance, the Dutchman Erasmus, said he had, "an astonishing knowledge of everything." Like Henry, James spoke several languages and was fascinated by the arts. He founded universities, and encouraged noblemen to send their children to school.

The Protestant Reformation

In Europe, meanwhile, trouble was brewing. A German monk named Martin Luther had begun to attack the Catholic Church, arguing that it needed to be reformed. His ideas soon became the basis for a new form of Christianity, called Protestantism.

Protestants claimed that the Church was rich and corrupt. They rejected the authority of the Pope, and believed that church services should be read in their own language, instead of Latin. Throughout Europe, Christians argued fiercely over religion.

Under the leadership of Henry and James, England and Scotland remained Catholic. But as books and pamphlets written by Protestants flowed into Britain, people began to move away from Catholicism. When Henry and James died, the next few years were dominated by struggles over whether England and Scotland would be Catholic or Protestant.

Printing ideas

New ideas spread fast, thanks to a method of printing, invented during the late Middle Ages by a German, Johannes Gutenberg.

His printing presses meant that books and pamphlets could be produced easily, and read aloud in public places.

During the Reformation, books helped to spread the word about Martin Luther and Protestantism.

Edward VI

This portrait shows Edward VI at six months old. He grew up to be an intelligent, serious boy, and oversaw big changes to the English Church.

Paintings, statues and stained glass windows were smashed or removed.

Church services were held in English, instead of Latin.

Thomas Cranmer, the Archbishop of Canterbury, introduced a Protestant prayer book to be used by everyone in England.

Religious turmoil

Henry VIII died in 1547, and the crown passed on to his nine-year-old son, who became Edward VI. Since Edward was so young, his uncle, the Duke of Somerset, was appointed to rule on his behalf. Under his uncle's influence, Edward made changes to the English Church, to bring it closer to the ideas of European Protestants.

The nine-day queen

But Edward became ill, and in 1553 he died, naming as his successor his 17-year-old Protestant cousin, Lady Jane Grey. When Jane was proclaimed Queen, Edward's Catholic half-sister Mary, who was next in line for the throne, was horrified. She gathered support, then marched to London, took power, and began preparing for her coronation. Jane was imprisoned in the Tower of London and later beheaded. She had been Queen for only nine days, and hadn't even been crowned.

A 19th-century painting of Lady Jane Grey's execution

Bloody Mary

As soon as she became Queen, Mary turned back the clocks. She made the Pope head of the English Church again, and freed Catholic priests whom Edward had imprisoned, locking up Protestant clergy instead. She also married a Catholic, the future King Philip II of Spain, despite many people's fears that this would give the Spanish power over England.

During the five years of Mary's reign, she had more than 300 Protestants burned alive at the stake. By the time she died in 1558, Mary was so unpopular among Protestants that they nicknamed her 'Bloody Mary' and celebrated the day of her death each year. Mary never had any children, so it was left to her Protestant half-sister, Elizabeth, to take the throne.

The Scottish Reformation

Meanwhile, north of the border, the Protestant Reformation swept through Scotland. At its head was a fiery preacher named John Knox, who attacked Catholicism in his sermons. In 1560, the Scottish Parliament voted in Protestantism as the country's official religion.

At this time, James IV's Catholic daughter, Mary, Queen of Scots, was living in France as the wife of the *Dauphin*, the heir to the French throne. It was here that she changed her name from 'Stewart' to 'Stuart' – to sound more French. When her husband died in 1560, Mary returned to her kingdom of Scotland, which had been ruled by her mother while she was away. But she found that her Catholic faith made her unwelcome. It seemed that in England and Scotland, the battle between Catholics and Protestants had been won by the Protestants – for now, at least.

Shown here in his clerical robes, John Knox was a fierce opponent of the Catholic Queen, and thought it was wrong for women to be monarchs.

Elizabeth I

Bloody Mary's half-sister Elizabeth was crowned Queen of England in 1558. The daughter of Henry VIII and Anne Boleyn, Elizabeth I became one of the most successful monarchs in European history. She was a brilliant politician and diplomat, and during her reign, England became an important European power. She made the country Protestant once again, but she didn't execute Catholics – unless they plotted against her.

Queen Elizabeth knew how important it was to look like a monarch. Here, courtiers carry her in a litter – a finely decorated, portable chair.

Elizabeth's courtiers

Elizabeth surrounded herself with a court of over 1,000 leading men, who flattered her with displays of dancing and recitals of love poetry. Some of them even kept their marriages secret, in case it upset her. These courtiers depended on Elizabeth for their wealth, as she could grant them land and titles. Those that she liked best, such as Robert Dudley, the Earl of Leicester, became very rich.

Elizabeth also made rules for her court, to create a strong image for the monarchy. Courtiers were never allowed to turn their backs on her. After speaking to her, they had to walk away backwards. Wherever the Queen went, trumpet fanfares announced her arrival.

Royal tours

Throughout her reign, Elizabeth went on regular tours, known as progresses, around the south of England, staying as a guest with chosen courtiers. She always made her host provide lavish entertainment for the entire court, saving her vast amounts of money. A visit from the Queen was a huge privilege, but it was so ruinously expensive that many courtiers dreaded her arrival.

The Virgin Queen

Elizabeth's chief advisors, known as the Privy Council, hoped that the Queen would marry and give birth to an heir. Many important men – including Philip II of Spain, her sister Mary's widower – wanted to win power by marrying her. But Elizabeth didn't want to share her position with anyone. Because she never married, she is sometimes called the Virgin Queen.

Royal beauty

Everyone wanted to look like the Queen. Women went to great lengths to copy her striking white makeup and red hair.

For the skin, they rubbed on a toxic mixture of white lead, vinegar and raw egg white. False veins were then painted on to make the skin look even paler.

They dyed or bleached their hair, or wore wigs – like Elizabeth herself.

Several of Elizabeth's teeth were rotten and black. Many women even copied this, rubbing their teeth with soot to make them black.

21

Elizabethan fashion

Queen Elizabeth probably got her dress sense from her father. He took great care over his appearance, and loved to dress up in fine clothing and jewels. But he became worried that some wealthy merchants were better dressed than his nobles – and he wanted everyone to be able to spot a noble. So he introduced new 'sumptuary laws' to control what clothing people wore. Nobles could wear materials and dyes that were banned for other people, however rich they were.

Young adults

Young boys and girls from noble families were dressed like small adults. Here, the children of Lady Tasburgh are dressed up to look just like Queen Elizabeth.

Their mother, standing at the back, is wearing an expensive black gown.

Dressed to impress

By the time of Elizabeth's reign, everyone wanted to show off by wearing elegant clothes. Elizabeth herself is said to have owned more than 250 gowns. A person's clothing was a way of displaying how rich and powerful they were. For instance, black dye was very expensive – so nobles wore black clothing so that people knew they were rich.

Dressed for work

While fashions moved quickly among nobles, little changed for the poorer people in society. Their clothes were made to work in, and so were much more practical. They were spun out of thick, itchy wool, and were usually brown, since this was the cheapest dye. Farmers often wore just a tunic, so they didn't get too hot.

Gentlemen of the court

Elizabeth's courtiers were the best dressed people in all of Britain. Male courtiers wore lots of layers, to make themselves look big and impressive. Some even wore shoulder pads and stuffed their clothing.

First they put on a shirt, and a coat called a doublet.

A jerkin went over the doublet.

A long gown or cloak went on top. This was often trimmed with fur.

On Sundays, every man wore a hat.

The doublet was fastened with laces. Buttons were just for decoration.

Ladies of the court

Ladies of the court were just as stylish as men. They dressed in richly embroidered gowns, made of heavy materials such as velvet. Underneath, they wore special undergarments to change the shape of their bodies.

A farthingale was a cone-shaped frame that pushed out the gown.

Many ladies wore a figure-hugging bodice to flatten their curves.

A pomander, a container of sweet-smelling spices, was hung from the waist.

Ladies had servants to help them dress.

Both men and women wore large, frilly collars called ruffs.

The Golden Age

Entertainment

In Tudor times, wealthy people enjoyed concerts, recitals, banquets and dancing.

At Elizabeth's court, art and culture flourished, and people called it a Golden Age. Poets such as John Donne and Edmund Spenser composed great works of literature. The Queen encouraged talented musicians to give concerts in private houses and playhouses. She also loved plays, and had performances put on at court specially for her entertainment.

Meanwhile, poorer people had their own entertainment. One common sport was bear baiting, in which people watched bears fighting with dogs.

People also held cock fights. Large bets were placed on which cock would win.

This picture shows Shakespeare's Globe playhouse with part of the wall cut away, so that you can see inside.

Plays became more and more popular during Elizabeth's reign. They were one of the few forms of entertainment that could be enjoyed by both rich and poor.

'Groundlings' pay a small price to stand and watch the play. Higher up, the seats are more expensive.

William Shakespeare

Elizabethan writers such as Christopher Marlowe and Ben Jonson produced brilliant plays that are still performed today. But the greatest writer of them all was William Shakespeare. He wrote at least 36 plays, acting in many of them, and he is now one of the most famous writers of all time.

Performances

Shakespeare put his plays on at the Globe, a playhouse in London that held up to 3,000 people. These performances were very different from modern productions. The actors had to shout to be heard over the noisy audience. Women were played by male actors wearing wigs and dresses. Actors in fight scenes used real weapons, and sometimes seriously injured each other. Cannons were sometimes fired on stage, and on one occasion, this set the building on fire.

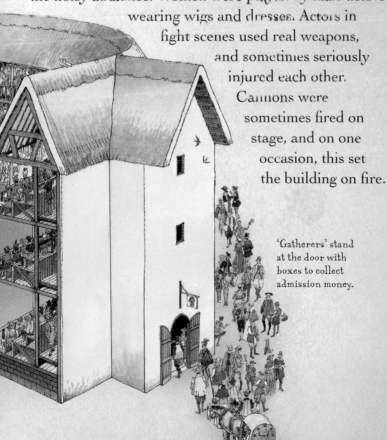

'Gatherers' stand at the door with boxes to collect admission money.

Shakespeare's plays

Shakespeare's plays included romances, such as *Romeo and Juliet*...

"O Romeo, Romeo! Wherefore art thou Romeo?"

Tragedies like *Hamlet*...

"To be, or not to be: that is the question."

And dramatic versions of British history, such as *Henry V*...

"Once more unto the breach, dear friends!"

Moving to the towns

The Poor Law

In England and Wales, the Elizabethan Poor Law made sure that all districts provided work for the poor, and shelter for those who couldn't work. The poor were divided into categories:

The 'impotent poor' were those who were considered too old, young or sick to work.

The 'able-bodied poor' were those who were unable to find work.

'Sturdy rogues' were those who could work but chose not to. They were thought to be lazy and dangerous, and were punished.

While Elizabeth's courtiers enjoyed new art, music and literature, life was getting harder for the poor people of England. The population had been rising during the Tudor period, and by the time of Elizabeth's reign, there weren't enough jobs to go around, especially in the countryside, where landowners were fencing off more and more land for their flocks of sheep.

Many people decided to pack their bags and head to the nearest town in search of employment. Swollen by these new arrivals, towns expanded rapidly, becoming dirty and overcrowded. Competition for jobs was fierce, and whole families were often forced into begging or stealing, just to stay alive.

Living in towns

Towns bustled with activity, and some people found work in new industries, such as glass and paper making, and book printing. Farmers could sell their produce in noisy open-air markets, and merchants traded all kinds of goods such as wool and iron. Exotic merchandise from all over the world flowed into ports such as London and Bristol – for the few who could afford it.

For most people, though, even soap was a luxury. There was no running water, and household waste was usually simply dumped in the street. Fleas, rats and flies were attracted to the crowded streets. The filth and vermin caused deadly diseases such as smallpox and tuberculosis to spread quickly. By 1600, London had a population of over 200,000. It was by far the biggest city in Britain, and one of the greatest trading cities in Europe. But it was also one of the filthiest places in the world.

Crime and punishment

With so many townspeople jobless and desperate for money, crime was common. There was no real police force in the 16th century, but local constables enforced laws, and town magistrates handed out harsh punishments. Anyone found begging without permission was flogged, murderers and thieves were hanged, nobles who were accused of treason were beheaded and people who spoke against the Church could be burned alive.

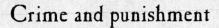

Dishonest people were locked in a wooden frame called a pillory, where people could throw things at them.

This picture shows a typical town in Elizabethan England.

It was against the law to kill large birds such as ravens. They were needed to eat the waste in the streets.

Streets are narrow and dirty.

This farmer has come to sell bales of wool.

The market

A pickpocket

Market stalls

Most buildings have tiled roofs and are made of wooden frames filled with plaster.

Exploring the world

In 1492, an Italian explorer named Christopher Columbus landed in America. At first, Europeans called it the New World, because they hadn't even known that it existed before. This was the start of a great age of European exploration. In 1498, the Portuguese explorer Vasco Da Gama found a sea route from Europe to the East Indies, which was rich with fine silks and spices.

Meanwhile, Spaniards were busy setting up colonies in the New World. By Elizabeth's time, their ships were sailing back and forth across the Atlantic Ocean, bringing home vast quantities of gold and silver from South and Central America, and the West Indies.

English adventurers

Envious of Spain's growing riches, Elizabeth encouraged her sailors to search for new lands and treasures too. Sir Walter Raleigh hunted for gold in South America, while Sir John Hawkins sailed from Africa to the New World, bringing African slaves to work in the West Indies.

Elizabeth also gave her sea captains permission to attack foreign treasure ships, although this made them very unpopular with the Spaniards.

This is a replica of Francis Drake's flagship, the *Golden Hinde*.

Exotic goods

Elizabethan explorers brought back exotic goods that had never been seen before in England.

Sir Walter Raleigh brought back potatoes...

...but at first people tried to eat them raw.

Sir John Hawkins brought back tobacco...

...but his servant saw him smoking and poured water on him, thinking his master was on fire.

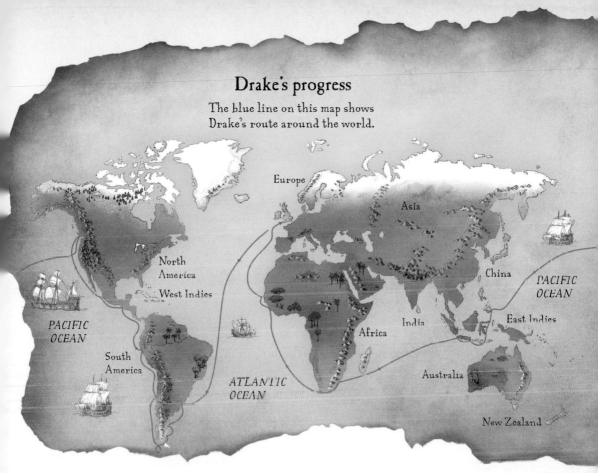

Drake's progress

The blue line on this map shows
Drake's route around the world.

Europe

Asia

North
America

China

PACIFIC
OCEAN

West Indies

PACIFIC
OCEAN

East Indies

India

South
America

Africa

ATLANTIC
OCEAN

Australia

New Zealand

Around the world

Among these captains was a man named Francis
Drake. He was so feared by the Spaniards that they
nicknamed him *El Draque* – the Dragon. To them he
was just a pirate. But to the English, he was a hero.

In 1577, Drake set sail across the Atlantic
Ocean, to plunder Spanish ships and settlements
in South and Central America. Some of his ships
were lost in stormy seas, but he continued on into
the Pacific Ocean, then to the East Indies and
Africa, before returning home laden with silver,
gold and pearls that he had looted from the
Spaniards. The journey took three years, but
Francis Drake had become the first Englishman
to sail all the way around the world.

Elizabeth came to meet
Drake on board the
Golden Hinde, where
he was knighted for
services to his country.

Rival queens

An early portrait of Mary, Queen of Scots. Catholic painters usually made her look beautiful, as she appears here, while Protestant artists made her look ugly.

In England, while Protestants were enjoying religious freedom, Catholics were being forced to pay fines, and were even banned from holding religious services. Most of them felt they could do nothing about this, but some were determined to turn England into a Catholic country again, and this meant replacing Elizabeth with a Catholic monarch. As it happened, there was an ideal candidate – Mary Stuart, Queen of Scotland, who was Elizabeth's cousin.

Mary in Scotland

When Mary took up power in Scotland in 1561, after the death of her French husband, the Scots were suspicious of her. They were fiercely Protestant, and were scared that Mary might try to impose her Catholic faith on them. Since she had spent most of her early years in France, they also saw her as a foreigner, who knew nothing of their country.

Mary soon won them over. She married a handsome Scottish nobleman Lord Darnley, and although she held Catholic services for herself, she made no attempt to interfere with the country's religion. For a while, her subjects were content – but that quickly changed.

A murder for a murder

Within months of her marriage, Mary discovered that the dashing Lord Darnley was little more than a bullying drunkard. He grew jealous of his wife, and angry at her close relationship with her secretary, David Rizzio.

In 1566, Darnley joined a plot to kill Rizzio, and helped to stab him to death. Mary never recovered from the shock of this murder, and grew to hate her husband. A year later, Darnley was strangled to death, and most people thought that Mary was involved. There was a scandal, and Mary had to abdicate, and flee to England.

Catholic plots

As soon as Mary arrived in England, Catholics began plotting to put her on the English throne. Elizabeth had no choice but to keep Mary locked up. Her ministers advised her to execute Mary, but Elizabeth didn't want to kill a queen – especially her own cousin.

One of these ministers, Sir Francis Walsingham, ran a network of spies to uncover plots. A firm Protestant, he was desperate to prove that Mary was guilty of treason. In 1586, one of his spies gave him a coded letter from Mary to a Catholic plotter, in which she agreed to have Elizabeth killed. This finally convinced the Queen of England to have her rival beheaded.

Mary's pet dog went with her to the execution, hidden under her dress.

The Babington Plot

Mary was executed in 1587 for her part in the Babington Plot, masterminded by a wealthy young Catholic, Anthony Babington.

Babington planned for Elizabeth to be murdered and for a Spanish army to invade England.

But among the plotters was one of Walsingham's spies. He revealed that the plotters were sending messages to each other hidden inside beer barrels.

Babington and his conspirators were imprisoned, and put to death. Soon after that, Mary was tried and executed at Fotheringhay Castle.

The Spanish Armada

Facing the Armada

Legend has it that when news reached England that the Armada was approaching, Sir Francis Drake was playing a game of bowls. He is supposed to have remarked casually, "we have time to finish this game, and beat the Spaniards too."

Elizabeth I delivered a great speech to the English army at Tilbury fort to encourage them to fight hard.

"I know I have but the body of a weak and feeble woman; but I have the heart of a king, and of a king of England, too."

Almost immediately after Mary's execution, Elizabeth faced another threat, this time from Philip II of Spain. He had become angry about English raids on Spanish ships in the Caribbean, especially as his spies had found that Elizabeth was taking a share of the treasure herself. To add to his fury, she was also helping Protestants in the Spanish-controlled Netherlands to rebel against him. Philip turned on the Queen whom he had once wanted to marry, and decided to go to war.

Plans of attack

In 1587, Philip planned to send a vast fleet of ships, known in Spanish as an *armada*, to the Netherlands. There it would pick up a Spanish army of 30,000 men, and ferry them over the English Channel to invade England. But there was an unexpected setback. English spies discovered Philip's plans, and Sir Francis Drake raided the Spanish port of Cadiz, where the Armada was assembling. There, he burned many ships before they had even set sail. It is said that Drake boasted that he had singed the King of Spain's beard.

Fire ships

When the Armada finally set sail in July 1588, it was met by an English fleet led by Lord Howard of Effingham, with Drake as his vice-admiral. They hounded the Spanish ships as they sailed up the English Channel. The Spaniards took shelter in the French port of Calais, but in the dead of night, the English set fire to eight of their own ships and sent them crashing into the enemy fleet. This drove the Spaniards into the open sea, where the English were waiting to attack them.

Victory

On August 8, 1588, the rival fleets met at the Battle of Gravelines, near Calais. The English destroyed several Spanish ships, but could not defeat the Armada entirely.

Then, the next day, strong winds drove the Spaniards north, before they had a chance to pick up Philip's army in the Netherlands. They were forced to sail around Scotland and Ireland and back to Spain, with storms wrecking many of their ships along the way. In London, crowds cheered as Elizabeth gave a speech, thanking God for the victory. Many Protestants saw their success as a sign that God was on their side.

The Armada in Ireland

→ Route of the Armada

◼ Spanish lands

Many Spanish ships were wrecked on the coast of Ireland. Around 5,000 Spaniards were drowned or killed by local Irishmen.

The English 'fire ships' were old or worn-out ships, loaded with firewood and tar. They caused little damage, but a lot of panic.

The cannons on the fire ships were loaded. There was no crew to fire them, but the flames set them off anyway.

England and Scotland remained two separate nations under James. But he was the first to use the term Great Britain, and he even created a new flag, the Union Jack, out of the English and Scottish flags.

A Stuart king

In 1603, the great Queen Elizabeth died without any children, and the Tudor dynasty came to an end. Her successor was James VI of Scotland, the son of Mary Stuart. Now, he was also James I, the first Stuart king of England. For the first time, Scotland, England, Ireland and Wales were all ruled by the same monarch.

James and the English

The English were excited about their new king, but James soon made himself unpopular by surrounding himself with Scottish courtiers, and tactlessly ignoring English customs.

To make matters worse, James was a fierce defender of the Divine Right of Kings. This was the idea that a king's power came from God, and nobody could question his decisions. His ideas offended members of Parliament, who wanted more power in government.

The Gunpowder Plot

James loved to lecture his subjects. He called himself the "great schoolmaster of the whole land" – and he hoped to convert everyone to his Protestant beliefs. This upset some Catholics, who were disappointed that the son of Mary Stuart would not let them worship in peace.

It wasn't long before a number of Catholics began plotting against the King.

One group came up with a particularly daring plan: to use gunpowder to blow up the Houses of Parliament, with James inside.

This portrait shows James in fine clothing. He was so scared of being assassinated that he had his clothing specially padded, in case he was stabbed.

A date to remember

But one of the conspirators warned a fellow Catholic, Lord Monteagle, to stay away from Parliament. Monteagle told the authorities at once. At midnight on the 5th of November, 1605, soldiers searched the cellars beneath the Houses of Parliament, and found Guido, or Guy, Fawkes, one of the conspirators, with barrels of gunpowder. The plotters were rounded up and hanged. The date went down in British history and is now celebrated every year with bonfires and fireworks.

Fighting with Parliament

Meanwhile, Parliament was getting more and more frustrated with the King, who loved to show off his royal power and fritter away money on his friends. This was especially offensive to a group of extreme Protestants known as Puritans, who thought that people should work hard and live a simple life. James's quarrels with Parliament grew more and more serious, and when his son, Charles, became King in 1625, the situation reached a crisis point.

Torture

After his arrest, Guy Fawkes was tortured in the Tower of London.

He was then made to sign his name on a confession, but was barely able to write.

Top: signature after torture
Below: signature 8 days later, after he recovered

This print shows the Gunpowder Plot conspirators. Their leader was Robert Catesby, who is second from the right. Guy Fawkes stands next to him.

Robert Winter · Christopher Wright · Iohn Wright · Thomas Percy · Guido Fawkes · Robert Catesby · Thomas Winter

King or Parliament

Charles I was a shy, dignified young man, who stammered when he spoke. Like his father, James, he believed firmly in the Divine Right of Kings, and relied on his friends for advice. This infuriated many MPs, who thought that the King should consult them on important matters.

The Puritans in Parliament were also worried that Charles wanted to make England Catholic again, since the King was married to the Catholic French princess Henrietta Maria. They grew even more concerned when Charles appointed his friend, William Laud, as Archbishop of Canterbury. Although he was a Protestant, Laud hated Puritans, and brought in grand church ceremonies that seemed Catholic in style.

Charles in charge

Soon after coming to the throne, Charles needed to raise money to fight wars in Europe. But Parliament refused to help him. For a while, the King angrily dismissed Parliament every time its members argued with him, or tried to get rid of his advisors. Eventually, he grew so fed up that he sent the MPs home for good.

From 1629 to 1640, Charles ruled and raised money without calling Parliament. But this 'eleven years' tyranny' ended when he tried to introduce Laud's church ceremonies in Scotland, together with a new prayer book. Unfortunately for Charles, most Scots were Presbyterians. Their beliefs were similar to those of the Puritans, and they hated Laud's grand style of Protestantism. They also objected to Charles interfering in their country, because they saw him as a foreigner.

The National Covenant

In churches all over Scotland, angry mobs rioted and attacked clergymen. Thousands vowed to fight religious change, and signed the National Covenant, a document which attacked Laud's ideas. Charles had lost control, and before long the Scots were threatening war. In 1640, the King was finally forced to recall Parliament, and ask for money to raise an army.

This portrait by van Dyke show Charles I elegantly dressed. Many MPs disapproved of his extravagance, which cost the country a lot of money.

Parliament's revenge

The new Parliament knew that the King needed its help, and exploited the situation. Laud was arrested, together with the Earl of Strafford, one of the King's chief advisors. A group of MPs, led by the devout Puritan John Pym, brought in laws to reduce the King's powers. One law required him to call Parliament every three years.

The road to war

Charles was enraged by these plans to limit his authority. In January, 1642, he burst into the House of Commons and demanded the arrest of Pym and the four other leading MPs who had opposed him. But they had been warned and had already escaped. Charles left London, raised an army of Royalist supporters and declared war. His opponents, the Parliamentarians, prepared to fight against him.

Throughout England, families, villages and towns decided which side to join. The Civil War had begun.

The Civil War

This map shows which areas mainly supported Parliament and which supported the King at the outbreak of war in 1642.

For seven years, bloody battles raged between the Parliamentarians and the Royalists. The war involved almost everyone in Britain, and many families were torn apart by arguments over which side to join. Most Puritans fought for Parliament, while Catholics were mainly Royalists. The city of London and the navy sided with Parliament, which gave its armies a huge advantage. They had the wealth of the capital at their disposal, and could move troops by ship – which was much faster than marching by land.

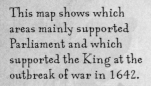

Marston Moor, 1644 ✕
Preston, 1648 ✕

✕ Naseby, 1645

Edgehill, 1642 ✕
Oxford ●
London ●

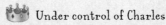 Under control of Parliament

👑 Under control of Charles

✕ Battle site and date

This scene shows a re-enactment of the Battle of Edgehill, the first battle of the Civil War.

Cavalrymen fought on horseback.

Foot soldiers fought with long, pointed wooden pikes.

Musketeers used guns called muskets, which were heavy and could be used as clubs in hand-to-hand fighting.

'Push of pike'

In battle, large blocks of soldiers with pikes advanced and tried to push the other side back. If one side broke, most of them would be killed.

Hedgehog

When enemy cavalry attacked, foot soldiers formed a 'hedgehog' with the musketeers in the middle and the pikemen around the edges.

The fight for London

The King raised his standard at Nottingham Castle to declare war, but as soon as it was up, a gust of wind blew it over. Many saw this as a bad omen. All the same, Charles set about preparing to fight. He made Oxford his base, gathered his army, and headed for London. He was determined to capture the capital.

The first big battle took place at Edgehill. The Royalists were helped by Charles's nephew, Prince Rupert of the Rhine, who was a brilliant cavalry commander. But the Parliamentarians managed to stop the King's army from reaching London.

Marston Moor

Meanwhile, Charles's enemy John Pym made a deal with the Scots. They would send an army to join forces with Parliament. In return, Parliament would establish the Presbyterian Church in England. In 1644, the combined Scottish and Parliamentarian army met the King's Cavaliers at Marston Moor. It was the biggest and bloodiest battle of the war. The Royalists lost, and Parliament won control of northern England.

Roundheads and Cavaliers

Royalists called the Parliamentarian soldiers Roundheads, because they cut their hair short and wore round helmets.

The Parliamentarians called their enemies Cavaliers, after the French word *chevalier*, meaning a knight. They thought that Cavaliers were vain and arrogant.

Oliver Cromwell

Oliver Cromwell was a Puritan who became MP for Huntingdon in 1628. When war broke out he joined the army, and rose rapidly through the ranks. He led the Parliamentarian cavalry at Marston Moor and at Naseby.

Victory and defeat

After the Battle of Marston Moor, the Royalists were all but defeated. Charles had missed his chance to capture London and win the war, and now he was running out of money. His soldiers were mostly local troops who did not want to travel too far away from their homes, and this meant that he couldn't move his armies around freely.

Meanwhile, the Parliamentarian army was getting even stronger. An MP named Oliver Cromwell persuaded Parliament to create a 'New Model Army' made up of professional soldiers, who were fiercer and tougher than the untrained Royalist troops.

In 1645 the New Model Army was put to the test, when it faced the King's army at the Battle of Naseby. Cromwell's soldiers crushed their opponents, and the Royalists fled.

The Battle of Naseby was the end for Charles. Soon afterwards he gave himself up to the Scots, hoping for protection – but in 1647, they handed him over to Parliament. It looked as if the war had been won.

Unlike Charles, the Puritan Oliver Cromwell did not want to be flattered in paintings. This portrait shows him 'warts and all' – with a red face and a shiny nose.

The second war

Charles had one last chance to snatch victory from the jaws of defeat. While he was imprisoned at Carisbrooke Castle on the Isle of Wight, the King persuaded the Scots to change sides and join the Royalists. But it was all in vain. In 1648, the final battle of the Civil War was fought at Preston. It was another resounding victory for the New Model Army.

The King on trial

The leaders of the New Model Army thought Charles was too dangerous to be kept alive. They saw his alliance with Scotland as treason, and argued that he should be put on trial. But Charles claimed that the courts had no right to try the King.

A vote was held in Parliament to decide whether there should be a trial. That day, Cromwell's soldiers surrounded the House of Commons, keeping out any MPs they thought would vote against trying the King. Cromwell and his allies had already decided on the verdict: Charles was sentenced to death, and the monarchy abolished.

On January 30, 1649, King Charles I was beheaded outside the Banqueting House in London. There was no rejoicing. As the blow fell, the crowd let out a huge groan. Many sobbed openly.

Rule by Parliament

For the first time in a thousand years, the country had no monarch. Instead, it was ruled by Parliament, led by Oliver Cromwell, who had risen from the middle classes to become the most powerful man in the land. His rule came to be known as the Commonwealth.

Trial and execution

No one wanted to be the man to sentence Charles to death. In the end, John Bradshaw reluctantly agreed to be judge at the King's trial.

Bradshaw was so scared of being assassinated that he wore this hat, lined with steel, to stop bullets.

The day of Charles's execution was freezing cold. Proud until the end, he asked for an extra shirt to wear, so the crowd wouldn't think he was shivering with fear.

The Commonwealth

Escape

After Cromwell won the Battle of Worcester, Charles Stuart had lots of adventures while trying to escape.

He cut his hair and pretended to be a woodsman.

He hid in 'priest-holes' – secret rooms in Catholic people's houses, used to hide priests in times of persecution.

He even spent a day hiding in an oak tree. Many pubs in England are named 'Royal Oak' in memory of Charles's hiding place.

Although the King was dead, there were still many Royalists in Ireland and Scotland who hoped to put his son, Charles Stuart, on the throne. Cromwell dealt with them swiftly and brutally.

First, he took the New Model Army to Ireland, and killed thousands of Irish Royalists, many of whom were Catholic. Meanwhile, Scottish Royalists crowned Charles King of Scotland, and invaded England. Cromwell returned from Ireland and crushed them at the Battle of Worcester. Charles himself managed to escape to France, where he stayed in exile, waiting for a chance to return.

Lord Protector

With his opponents defeated, Cromwell gave himself the title of 'Lord Protector' and ruled England for five years, until his death in 1658. Just like Charles I before him, he often argued with Parliament and dismissed it. Unlike Charles, though, he had a powerful army on his side.

In 1655 there was yet another Royalist uprising, and Cromwell decided that he needed to keep a closer watch over his people. He divided England into 11 districts, each one ruled by a major-general. Then he set about enforcing Puritan values all over the land. He closed down inns and playhouses, and banned popular pastimes such as bear-baiting and traditional activities, including maypole dancing. People were fined for being drunk, for gambling, and even for playing sports.

Life under Cromwell

Most people were scared of Cromwell's army, and hated the dull Puritan lifestyle. The Lord Protector even banned Christmas and Easter celebrations, and replaced them with days of fasting.

But in many other ways life got much better. For one thing, Cromwell allowed people to worship in almost any way they wished. For another, many people were becoming richer, as overseas trade thrived – especially the trade in sugar and slaves with the West Indies.

When Cromwell died, his son Richard became Lord Protector. But Richard had nothing like his father's character, and he couldn't control Parliament or the army. Before long, the army took matters into its own hands, and invited Charles I's son back from exile in France, to become King Charles II. Oliver Cromwell had worked hard to make England into what he saw as a better place. But after his strict Puritan Commonwealth, almost everyone was excited about having a king on the throne again.

Cromwell stripped churches of decoration – paintings, statues and stained glass windows.

His soldiers even raided people's houses to take away their Christmas dinner.

This painting shows the Puritan family of Henry Chorley, a cloth merchant from Preston. Puritans wore simple, plain clothes, unlike the extravagant outfits of Charles I's court.

Daniel his   Samuel his

The Merry Monarch

Charles II couldn't have been more different from Cromwell. A fun-loving king, he soon earned the nickname the Merry Monarch. He was cultured too, and encouraged science, art, drama and music to flourish. Charles introduced champagne to Britain, reopened the playhouses that Cromwell had banned, and sparked a fashion for sailing when he and his brother raced their yachts down the River Thames.

Care-free and heir-free

The King was charming and good-looking, with an eye for the ladies. He was married to a Portuguese princess, Catherine of Braganza, but had a string of affairs with many different women. His mistresses produced 14 children between them, but none of them could be heir to the throne. The Queen didn't have any children, so Charles would be succeeded by his brother, James.

Crime pays

In 1671, a man named Colonel Blood disguised himself as a priest and tried to steal the Crown Jewels. When he was caught, he demanded to see the King.

Charles was so impressed by his bravery and his amusing stories that he not only pardoned him, but rewarded him with a pension and some land.

Problems with Parliament

At the beginning of his reign, Charles was careful
to build a good relationship with Parliament,
because he didn't want to risk another civil war.
But soon he began to clash with MPs over religion.
They wanted to make sure that the country would
remain Protestant, and many believed that Charles
was secretly a Catholic. Charles was certainly
sympathetic to Catholics – he was trying to persuade
Parliament to give them more rights, and his brother
had converted to Catholicism.

   Then, in 1670, Charles made a secret deal with
Louis XIV of France. In exchange for money, he
promised to become a Catholic and to help the
French in their war against the Dutch. When gossip
about the deal spread through Parliament, many MPs
felt that Charles couldn't be trusted.

Party politics

James was even less
popular than his
brother, and some MPs
were determined to stop
him from succeeding to
the throne. Politicians
became so divided on the
matter that they formed
two political parties.

The MPs who supported
James were called Tories,
and those who were
against him were called
Whigs. They were the
first political parties
in Britain.

This painting shows Charles entering
London the day before his coronation. He is
wearing a tall hat and riding a white horse.

In this picture, the plague is depicted as a skeleton dancing on coffins, with London in the background.

"Ring a ring o' roses
Pocket full o' posies
Atishoo! Atishoo!
We all fall down."

This nursery rhyme is said to be about the Black Death. Victims would show symptoms such as red rashes on the body ("ring o' roses") and sneezing ("Atishoo!") before falling down – dead.

The plague

When Charles came to the throne, London was a dirty, overcrowded city. Rats thrived in the grimy conditions, and diseases spread very easily. In the summer of 1665, just four years into Charles' reign, London was ravaged by a deadly disease called the Bubonic Plague.

The plague germs were carried by fleas which lived in the fur of black rats. Fleas passed the plague, also known as the Black Death, to humans when they bit them. Within days of being bitten, black blotches and huge, painful lumps would appear on victims' bodies. Sometimes their fingers, toes and noses turned black and fell off. They would writhe in agony for days, vomiting and shaking, before they finally died.

"Bring out your dead!"

Nobody knew what caused the plague, or how to cure it, so anyone who showed symptoms was locked in their house with their family, and left to die. A red cross was painted on the door to warn others to stay away. Many people starved, as they could not leave their houses to find food. At night, men would roam the streets with huge carts, crying, "Bring out your dead!" Corpses were loaded up and driven away to enormous burial pits on the outskirts of the city.

Eventually, the cold winter weather killed off the fleas, and the plague began to die down. But the Black Death had killed 68,000 Londoners – around one in five of the population.

Doctors wore leather robes with hoods and gloves. Their masks had glass eyeholes and beaks stuffed with herbs, which were supposed to protect them from the plague.

Samuel Pepys

Much of what we know about the plague comes from the diary of Samuel Pepys. He was an MP and an administrator for the navy. He wrote in his diary almost every day between 1660 and 1669, and kept detailed notes on everything from his private life to public events, including the coronation of Charles II.

Pepys's diary tracks the spread of the plague, and gives a very personal account of the tragedy. On August 10, 1665, he rushed home to write his will, realizing that, "a man cannot depend upon living two days to an end." But by September 3, he was more concerned that his new wig would go out of fashion: "for nobody will dare to buy any hair for fear of the infection, that it had been cut off the heads of people dead of the plague."

Extracts from Samuel Pepys' Diary

June 7, 1665

This day...I did in Drury Lane see two or three houses marked with a red cross upon the doors, and "Lord have mercy upon us" writ there – which was a sad sight to me, being the first of that kind that to my remembrance I ever saw

October 16, 1665

Lord, how empty the streets are, and melancholy, so many poor sick people in the streets, full of sores, and so many sad stories overheard as I walk, everybody talking of this dead, and that man sick.

November 22, 1665

I heard this day that the plague is come very low; that is 600 and odd – and great hopes of a further decrease, because of this day's being a very exceeding hard frost – and continues freezing.

London's burning

Just as people started to feel safe in London again, a second disaster struck. In the early hours of September 2, 1666, a fire started in a bakery on Pudding Lane, in the heart of the city. It was a hot, dry summer, with strong winds that fanned the flames. The Great Fire, as it became known, raged for four days, destroying four-fifths of London.

Panic spreads

At first, no one thought the fire was very serious. Sir Thomas Bludworth, the Lord Mayor of London, was irritated when he was woken in the middle of the night and told about the fire. 'Pish!' he said and, thinking the fire would be easy to put out, he went back to bed. But as he slept, the fire raged on. By morning, hundreds of houses had already been destroyed.

Most of the shops and houses in London were made of wood, and they were tightly packed together, so it was easy for the flames to spread. There was no fire service, and very few people had water in their homes to throw on the flames. Panic-stricken Londoners rushed to the river to fill buckets with water, but the fire was impossible to control.

> "The stones of St. Paul's flew like grenades, the lead melting down the streetes in a stream, & the very pavements glowing with fiery redness, so as nor horse nor man was able to tread on them."

John Evelyn, a writer and gardener, describes the destruction of St. Paul's Cathedral during the Great Fire of London in his diary.

Londoners flee to the south side of the river to escape the flames, throwing their belongings into boats, in the hope that they'll survive the fire.

Tearing down the houses

King Charles insisted on pulling down as many buildings as possible to stop the fire from spreading to the Tower of London. The city's supply of gunpowder was kept there. If the fire had reached it, the consequences could have been catastrophic.

In the midst of the chaos, Pepys bumped into the Lord Mayor in the street, now wide awake. Pepys wrote that he cried, like a fainting woman, "Lord, what can I do? I am spent: people will not obey me. I have been pulling down houses, but the fire overtakes us faster than we can do it."

Lucky escape

Officially, only nine people died in the fire, but it is likely that there were many other deaths which went unrecorded.

The aftermath

By September 6, the fire had died down, and shaken Londoners began to return to the city.

But there was a silver lining to this tragedy: the fire killed the last of the rats and fleas which were carrying the plague, so the city was finally free of the Black Death.

This painting shows the Tower of London glowing in the light of the flames. Luckily, the fire never reached the Tower.

Wealthy Stuarts

Charles was determined to prevent such a fire from happening again, and so he ordered London to be rebuilt with stone, instead of wood. The architect Sir Christopher Wren was commissioned to design the new-look London. Narrow, winding streets were to be replaced with wide, paved avenues, but many of the plans had to be scrapped as there wasn't enough money to cover the costs. Even so, London was transformed. The most famous new landmark was Wren's magnificent St. Paul's Cathedral.

This portrait of Sir Christopher Wren shows St. Paul's Cathedral in the background. The arches and domes are in the Baroque style, influenced by Italian Renaissance architects.

The rich get richer

This new London reflected the newfound opulence of England under Charles II. While life for the poor remained much the same, life for the wealthy was improving rapidly. After the dull lifestyle of the Commonwealth, those who could afford it took advantage of their new freedom.

Clothing became more elaborate, with large wigs and bright coats for men, and beautiful gowns and lace for ladies. Furniture was more finely carved, and upholstered with leather. For the first time, many houses were designed with separate rooms for living, eating and sleeping in. Charles's court, meanwhile, developed a taste for all things French – from clothing to art.

Charles II in his finery. Men's clothing was similar to the clothing of Charles I's court, except that boots were replaced with stockings and buckled shoes.

50

Business booms

Trade flourished in the Stuart period, and a flurry of innovations made business easier. Envelopes, newspapers and insurance were all introduced for the first time. 1694 marked the foundation of the Bank of England (which was established to lend money to the government), and the appearance of the first English banknote.

In the early 1600s, coffee arrived in Britain. Coffee houses began springing up in cities from around 1650, and coffee gradually took over from beer as the nation's most popular drink. Coffee houses were soon fashionable places for men to meet and conduct business. At one point, Charles tried to close them all down, as he feared that plotters would use them as meeting places. But his subjects complained so bitterly that he relented.

This painting shows fashionable Stuart men socializing at a coffee house.

Trade triangle

Britain's wealth was largely thanks to booming trade overseas. The 'trade triangle' was most valuable. British merchants traded iron and guns for African slaves, and then sold them in the New World. Meanwhile, British ships brought home sugar, cotton and tobacco.

→ iron and guns
→ African slaves
→ sugar, cotton and tobacco

House and garden

How does your garden grow?

Herb gardens were usually planted in geometric beds and included plants which people believed to have medicinal properties. Here are a few plants that were popular in the 17th century, and the complaints they were supposed to cure:

The bitter herb wormwood was believed to keep away fleas and to relieve gout.

An infusion of marigolds was drunk to soothe the spirits.

Borage was said to drive away sorrow.

Feverfew was taken for headaches.

Bachelor's buttons buttercups were believed to cure insanity.

For an average, well-off family in the mid-17th century, life revolved around the home. The father of the household often ran his business from a shop or workshop on the ground floor, and the mother looked after the running of the house. Children spent less time at home than their parents, as they were usually sent to be educated at a grander family's house. At midday, the whole household would come together in the wood panelled main room, or hall, to eat a large meal, and they would eat a lighter supper in the evening.

Houses were lit by fire and candlelight. Candles were very expensive, and few people could afford good quality beeswax candles. Most of the time they used cheap tallow candles, made of animal fat, which smelled unpleasant and filled the house with smoke.

Pretty but practical

Richer people had gardens, which provided a welcome escape from the filth and bustle of the town. Most gardens had decorative flowers and trees, and some had ornamental features such as fountains or sundials.

Many of the plants grown had practical uses, too – vegetables were grown alongside herbs for cooking and medicinal purposes. A garden also served as a place where laundry could be hung out to dry, firewood and water could be stored, and pens could be built to house pigs or chickens to provide extra food for the family.

This is an illustration of a cloth merchant's house from around 1640. It has been cut away to reveal the different rooms and furnishings inside.

Servants lived in basic rooms known as garrets at the top of the house.

Bed chambers were often used for entertaining as well as sleeping.

The toilet, or privy, was housed in a shed behind the house. Waste went into a pit underneath, which was emptied at night by men called night soil men.

Isaac Newton

Sir Isaac Newton was the first person to suggest that science and mathematics could explain everything.

It is said that he came up with his theory of gravity when he saw an apple falling from a tree.

Newton also made important discoveries about light, and invented the mirror telescope to study the stars.

Newton's telescope

The rise of science

When the Great Fire happened so quickly after the plague, many people thought that it was the work of the devil – or a terrible punishment from God. In Stuart times, most people had to rely on religion, superstition or plain guesswork to try to explain the world around them. But, at the same time, intellectuals were making exciting scientific discoveries. Their work would have a huge impact on modern science.

The Royal Society

In the 1640s a group of scientists, including Christopher Wren and Samuel Pepys, began meeting to discuss ideas and perform experiments. They called themselves the Invisible College. By the 1660s, King Charles had officially recognized their work, and they became the Royal Society. Charles was so interested that he even helped out with some of the experiments. In 1675, he also set up the Royal Observatory in Greenwich, where astronomers studied the Sun, moon and stars. Their work was interesting, but it was also useful. For example, studying the stars helped them to tell the time and navigate at sea.

A true genius

In 1703, the Royal Society appointed a new president – Sir Isaac Newton, one of the greatest scientists of all time. One of his most important discoveries was that a force, which we call gravity, pulls objects towards the ground. He realized that gravity was what keeps the moon moving around the Earth. Newton was the first person to be knighted for scientific work.

Medicine

While Newton and the Royal Society were studying the natural world, doctors were learning more about the human body. Until the 1600s, little had been known about how the body worked, or what caused disease – the Church wouldn't allow dead bodies to be cut up and examined. Only one in ten people lived to be 40. Operations were done by 'barber surgeons' who set broken bones, as well as trimming hair. One common treatment was bleeding: cutting patients open to let out the 'bad blood' that they believed caused illness.

However, in the early 17th century, the Church finally allowed doctors to cut up corpses to learn more about the body. A physician named William Harvey made one of the most important medical discoveries of all, when he uncovered the secret of circulation. He realized that the heart is a pump, which makes blood flow around the body. Unfortunately, it took a long time for discoveries like this one to have a real impact, and treatments such as bleeding carried on long after Harvey's death.

Witch hunts

Despite new scientific knowledge, many people still believed in witches. In the 1640s, a lawyer named Matthew Hopkins came up with a test to identify witches. The accused was thrown into water. If she drowned, she was innocent. If she lived, she was thought to be a witch, and executed.

Inventions

Some Stuart inventions opened the way for a new industrial age.

1701 – Jethro Tull's seed drill plants seeds faster than by hand.

1705 – Thomas Newcomen's steam engine pumps flood water out of coal mines.

1709 – Abraham Darby discovers how to purify coal to make coke. Coke is used as a fuel in steel and iron production.

This painting by the Dutch artist Rembrandt shows some 17th century doctors examining the arm of a dead man.

A Catholic king

Charles II's extravagant lifestyle eventually caught up with him, and he died in 1685. He was succeeded by his brother James, who believed that God had put him on the throne to convert the country back to Catholicism. James refused to compromise with Parliament on matters of religion, and it wasn't long before this made him extremely unpopular with Protestant politicians – and the public.

This is a portrait of James II, wearing a curly wig that would have been the height of fashion at the end of the 17th century.

The Monmouth rebellion

Just four months into James's reign, the Protestant Duke of Monmouth – an illegitimate son of Charles II – led a rebellion against him, and tried to seize the crown. James's troops quashed the rebels, but it was a hollow victory. Monmouth was executed along with 300 other Protestant rebels, and a further 800 were shipped to Barbados as slaves. The brutal trials became known as the 'Bloody Assizes'. The King's harsh treatment of the defeated rebels made him more unpopular than ever.

Challenging the Church

In 1687, James tried to take the law into his own hands, issuing an order called the Declaration of Indulgence to abolish the laws against Catholics. Parliament refused to accept it, which made the King look weak and foolish, but he wouldn't give in.

He ordered the Declaration to be read out in every church, and when the bishops protested, he put them on trial. James was humiliated once again when his judges found the bishops not guilty.

The final blow

At first, James's critics could console themselves with the thought that he wouldn't be around for long. James was 52 when he came to the throne – an old man by the standards of the day – and, when he died, his Protestant daughter Princess Mary would be Queen. But, in 1688, everything changed. James's Catholic second wife, Mary of Modena, gave birth to a son named James. There was a new Catholic heir to the throne, and the Protestants were horrified.

Almost immediately, a group of MPs invited Princess Mary's Dutch husband, the Protestant Prince William of Orange, to invade. So, on November 5, 1688, William landed in Torbay with 15,000 men, forcing James to step down. James fled to France, and William and Mary were crowned King and Queen. This dramatic takeover became known as the Glorious Revolution.

The baby and the warming pan

Some people refused to accept that James's son was really his. Gossip spread that the baby had been smuggled into the Queen's bedroom in a warming pan.

This is a Dutch painting showing William of Orange landing in Torbay.

William and Mary

William and Mary were appointed by Parliament to
reign together. This put an end once and for all to the
idea that kings and queens were appointed by God. In
1689, they agreed to limit the powers of the monarchy,
with a Bill of Rights presented to them by Parliament.
It stated that all future monarchs had to be Protestant,
and that they couldn't keep an army or raise taxes
without permission from Parliament, which would have
to be called every three years.

"She seems to be
of a good nature...
she takes nothing
to heart; whilst the
Prince her husband
has a thoughtful
countenance, is
wonderfully serious
and silent, and seems
to treat all persons
alike gravely"

John Evelyn gives his
impression of William
and Mary in his diary.

The unpopular Dutchman

Mary was well-loved by the British people, but William
soon made himself unpopular. He made no secret of
the fact that he only wanted the throne so that British
soldiers would fight in a war he was waging against the
French. He spent most of his reign fighting in Europe,
leaving Mary to rule alone.

The exile returns

The exiled James II still had support – especially among Catholics in Ireland and Scotland – and saw that he had one last opportunity to reclaim his crown. In 1689, he landed in Ireland and, with the help of French and Irish Catholics, tried to seize control from the English Protestants who had settled there. He managed to hold the town of Derry under siege, but his army was no match for William's disciplined troops. On July 1, 1690, William defeated him at the Battle of the Boyne. What's more, the King gave more land in Northern Ireland to the English Protestants, and Derry was renamed Londonderry. Beaten, James II fled to France and lived there in exile for the rest of his life.

Highland massacre

William didn't want to risk another rebellion. So, in 1692, he made the Catholic clans (families) of the Scottish Highlands sign an oath of loyalty to him. When the MacDonalds of Glencoe missed the deadline to sign, 38 members of their clan were massacred by a rival clan, the Campbells, under orders from the government.

William alone

In 1694, Mary died of smallpox, leaving William to rule alone. William was devastated by his wife's death, and said he had never found a single fault in her. As they had no children, Parliament passed an Act of Settlement in 1701, declaring that Mary's sister, Anne, and her heirs, would succeed to the throne. A year later, William died and Anne became Queen.

A shaky start

William and Mary's marriage did not begin happily. Mary was only 15 when her father forced her to marry William, who was 12 years older than her

At nearly 1.8m (6 feet) tall, she towered over William, and she is said to have cried all the way through the wedding ceremony. But, against the odds, the couple gradually grew to love each other.

When William died in 1702, he was wearing Mary's wedding ring and a lock of her hair close to his heart.

The last Stuart

Queen Anne was a shy woman, whose reign was blighted by health problems and personal sadness. She was married to Prince George of Denmark, and was frequently pregnant, which made her health even worse. Anne gave birth to 19 children, but sadly none of them survived.

Queen Anne suffered from gout – a painful disease which causes swelling in the joints – so she was rarely seen in public.

She had an attack of gout during her coronation, and had to be carried in a sedan chair.

A challenge for Churchill

Early in Queen Anne's reign, Britain joined with Austria and the Netherlands in a war against France and Spain. A young general named John Churchill helped win a series of victories for the British, and became a national hero. Queen Anne rewarded him with a title, Duke of Marlborough, and a plot of land, where he built a palace called Blenheim, named after one of his most famous battles. His wife Sarah was Anne's closest friend, but eventually the two women fell out, and the Queen banished Churchill from public life.

Many generations of the Churchill family lived at Blenheim Palace. Sir Winston Churchill, Prime Minister during the Second World War, was born here in 1874.

The United Kingdom

It soon became clear that Anne would die without any children to succeed her. As some Scottish people still didn't accept the Act of Settlement, Parliament feared that the Scots might try to put James II's son, also called James, on the throne in Scotland. To prevent this, Parliament passed the Act of Union. In 1707, England, Scotland and Wales were united under one Parliament, and from then on the nation became known as the United Kingdom of Great Britain.

A new royal family

In 1714, Queen Anne died and the throne passed to the next in line: George, the son of Princess Sophia of Hanover, in Germany, and a great-grandson of James I. Parliament had become stronger during the Tudor and Stuart period, and the powers of the monarchy had gradually declined. But the country George now inherited was one of the most powerful in the world.

Index

Acknowledgements

Every effort has been made to trace and acknowledge ownership of copyright. If any rights have been omitted, the publishers offer to rectify this in any future editions following notification. The publishers are grateful to the following individuals and organizations for their permission to reproduce material on the following pages: (t=top, b=bottom, l=left, r=right)

Cover (main) Woburn Abbey, Bedfordshire, UK/Bridgeman, (ml) Private Collection, The Stapleton Collection/Bridgeman, (background) Risglitz/Hulton Archive/Getty Images; p1 The Art Archive/ Magdalene College Cambridge/Eileen Tweedy; p2-3 © Museum of London; p6 (t) © Stapleton Collection/Corbis; p8 © AKG, London; p10-11 © Patrick Ward/Corbis; p12-13 Musee de la Marine, Paris, France, Lauros/Giraudon/Bridgeman; p15 Hoefnagel, Joris (1542-1600)/Hatfield House, Hertfordshire, UK/Bridgeman; p16 Hans Holbein, The Ambassadors © The National Gallery, London; p18 (tl) © The Art Archive/ National Gallery of Art Washington/Album/Joseph Martin, (b) Paul Delaroche, The Execution of Lady Jane Grey © The National Gallery, London; p19 (br) © Towneley Hall Art Gallery and Museum, Burnley, Lancashire/Bridgeman; p20 © The Stapleton Collection/Bridgeman; p22 © The Gallery Collection/Corbis; p25 (tr) © Chris Hellier/Corbis; p28 (b) © Joel W. Rogers/ Corbis; p30 The Royal Collection © 2008, Her Majesty Queen Elizabeth II; p34 (bl) © Christie's Images/Corbis; p35 (t) Private Collection/Bridgeman; (b) © Bettmann/ Corbis; p37 © Louvre, Paris, France, Lauros/Giraudon/Bridgeman; p38 (b) © Nigel and Linda Hillyard of actiontake1.com; p40 © The Art Archive/Pitti Palace, Florence; p41 (r) © Ashmolean Museum, University of Oxford, UK/Bridgeman; p43 (b) © Harris Museum and Art Gallery, Preston, Lancashire, UK/ Bridgeman; p44-45 © Museum of London, UK/Bridgeman; p46 (tl) © Bodleian Library, University of Oxford, Plague skeleton from Thomas Dekker's A Rod for Run-aways, 1625, Reference Mal. 601(l), (bl) © Bettman/Corbis; p47 © Bettmann/Corbis; p50 (tl) © Private Collection/ Bridgeman, (b) © The Art Archive/Christ's Hospital/Eileen Tweedy; p51 (b) © The Art Archive/ British Museum/Eileen Tweedy; p52-53 © John Ronayne/Geffrye Museum; p54 (tl) Academie des Sciences, Paris, France, Lauros/Giraudon/Bridgeman, (bl) © The Art Archive/British Museum/Eileen Tweedy; p55 (tr) Mary Evans Picture Library, (b) © Bettman Corbis; p56 © National Maritime Museum; p57 (b) The Royal Collection © 2008, Her Majesty Queen Elizabeth II; p58 (t) © Massimo Listri/Corbis; p60 (tl) © PhilipMould, Historical Portraits Ltd., London, UK/Bridgeman; p60-61 © Jarrold Publishing, reproduced by kind permission of the publisher.

Digital design by John Russell. Picture research by Ruth King.